Strut Thru It

STRUT YOUR WAY TO A HAPPIER YOU

Mantra Journal

BY

LOLITA FRAZIER

Printed in the United States of America

First Edition, 2022
ISBN 978-1-0880-2385-3

Red Pen Edits and Consulting, LLC
P. O. Box 25283
Columbia, SC 29223
www.redpeneditsllc.com

Table Of Contents

Dedications

I dedicate this book to my beautiful mother, Joyce Frazier. Mom, I just want to thank you for showing me not only how to love but how to forgive. Thank you for your love, guidance and protection even in the midst of your own storms. Your love has shown me the way. You were the first person to be the example of what grace and struttin' thru it looked like. It's because of your love for us, that we love our children with everything in us. It's because of you that I stand firm in my truth accepting the good, the bad and the ugly, while staying focused on the brighter days. You will forever be my first love.

Love Cola

Walk In It Or Strut Thru It, - The Choice Is Yours

One of the hardest things to do during a storm imagining what coming out on the other side looks like or feels like. We get so consumed with the emotions that we are feeling in that very moment that it can feel like we are being held hostage to what we're going through. Instead of allowing these challenges to consume us, we must start looking at them in a more positive light - understanding that these challenges, are simply life's lessons

These are the times to dig deep within us and to uncover the power that each one of us possesses. Struttin' through a situation can be as simple as changing your posture. Did you know that body language can communicate the feelings or emotions a person is feeling even when they think they are hiding it? Have you ever had someone walk up to you and randomly ask you "is everything ok"? Or how about have someone say "Smile. It is not that bad"? Well, believe it or not these questions may not be so random or asked by coincidence. This is the nonverbal conversation that your body is having with the world. I call it "Strut Talk" - the conversation with no words. Body language does not only influence our physical body and posture, but it can also mentally and emotionally intensify how we are feeling.

If you are experiencing negative feelings such as hurt, pain, anger, depression, etc, your posture may be slouched. Your shoulders and head may be down. There is a lack of eye contact which could cause you to come across as someone who is bitter, uninterested or does not care and that may not be the case at all. This is called **"Walking in it**." Experiencing these same feelings, we can change the conversation as well as how we feel and are perceived by others by changing our posture to reflect confidence and strength. Once that's done, our minds will follow. When tough times surface, we need to remain tall, with our shoulders rolled back our, our chin up, our core tight and our mind right, knowing that it is hard to be down when you are standing tall.

This is how you **"Strut Thru It"**!

Daily Exercise - "Walk It Out"

Step 1: Each participant will write down three feelings/emotions that they have experienced this week/month on pieces of paper.

Step 2: Fold them into small pieces. Place them in a box and give it a shake.

Step 3: Have the first participant select an emotion (Look but do not tell your emotion)

Step 4: Without using words, walk out the feeling or emotions using your posture, body language and eye contact only!

Step 5*:* Have remaining participants guess the "feeling/emotion" that you are walking out. Continue guessing until someone is able to call out the correct feeling/emotion. The person who guesses the correct feeling/emotion will then choose next. Repeat Steps 1-4.

Step 6: Create a journal entry explaining how this made you feel

Strut Talk

Date _____

We All Have A Story!
What Does Your Strut Say About You?

Would you believe me if I told you that your walk is the first conversation that you have with the world?

Without saying any words our body language, facial expressions, and overall demeanor tell our story in that moment. We all have a past. Oftentimes, we do not take the necessary steps to heal from our trauma. Instead, we just "grow up" allowing those negative thoughts and feelings to live and grow inside of us. I can remember growing up without my dad, and how I allowed those feelings of abandonment and rejection to carry over into my adulthood. I blamed this situation for most of my downfalls. I walked in this pain for years, but it wasn't until I forgave my dad that my entire life changed. We must realize that our lives are on purpose. These are the chapters that mold us into the person that we are today.

Not having a dad allows me to connect with other young girls who deal with the same situation. Because of this common ground, I'm able to relate and use my situation to help change someone else's life. Regardless of what caused you hurt, pain, trauma and uncertainty in your life, consider the purpose. Why did you have to go through it? Look at those issues as chapters. There are some things that we go through in life, that ultimately, are not about us at all. Its purpose is for us to be able to uplift, encourage, and save someone else from making the same mistakes or decisions. Today, be thankful for your story. Be thankful for the ups and the downs and everything that falls

Daily Exercise - "Strut Talk"

Step 1: Imagine not being able to have a verbal conversation and that your only form of communication is your Strut.

Step 2: Write down what you *think* your strut says about you.

Step 3: Write down what you *want* your strut to say about you

Step 4: Compare the results of Step 2 and Step 3.

Step 5: Create a journal entry detailing the comparison

Strut Talk

Date _____

Now Is The Time!

TODAY IS THE DAY!! Yes, I am talking to **YOU**. As you prepare to strut in your greatness, the only thing that you should be focused on is the "**NOW**"! It's the only time that matters. It is time for YOU to stop putting YOUR hopes and dreams on hold. It is time for YOU to stop waiting for things to be perfect when in all actuality..... the time is **NOW**!

It is time to stop procrastinating with **YOUR** life!

We have allowed our past and society to put a time stamp on when our greatness should be achieved based on several factors: too young to get started, too old to complete it, or perhaps simply feeling like our time is up. We must eliminate those limited beliefs that were forced into our lives and ask ourselves the question, "do I believe that is too late or has the world made me feel this way?"

If you are reading this, it confirms that you still can pursue your passions, fulfill your hopes, and make your dreams a reality.

Today is the perfect day! Start that new project. Mend a relationship. Break that bad habit. Make that decision you have been avoiding. It may be something simple like trying a new hairstyle/restaurant, etc. (You get the point.) Stop dwelling on the past and focus on this new day. A new day to plant seeds and watch them grow. A new day to start fresh. In this moment, nothing else matters. Make the commitment to yourself to do it NOW!

Daily Exercise - Create A Dream Board

Step 1: Find a quiet space to sit, relax and reflect.

Step 2: Take a deep breath. Close your eyes. Imagine what your happiness and success look like.

Step 3: In your Journal, write down what you envisioned.

Step 4: Take a moment to find and save your images to create a Vision Board

Step 5: Place your Vision Board in a space that is visible as a reminder that NOW is the time

Strut Talk

Date _____

Keep Struttin' - You're Almost There

Have you ever felt like you were working backwards or at a standstill while trying to pursue your dreams or goals? Have you ever tried your hardest to stay focused, motivated, and positive, but things just never go your way?

This is something that many of us struggle with daily. We find ourselves working endlessly towards something that means so much, but things just don't seem to be moving fast enough or the way that we envisioned. In these moments, it is easy to lose sight of our progress because we put the focus on what has set us back instead of on what is needed to help us come up.

Instead of beating yourself up or allowing frustration to take over and really put your progress on hold these are the times to boost yourself up!

Did You Know That?

Repeating daily affirmations, uplifting quotes or positive mantras such as this will help change your mentality about your situation. When you speak nice to yourself, your mind releases the stress or negative feelings, and your body will automatically follow. These are the perfect moments to allow your creativity to flow. This will allow your mind and heart to connect. Lastly, this will remind yourself of how far you have come without focusing on how far you must go. Things happen for people when they are supposed to happen. It is all part of the plan. You must put in the work, remain consistent, and never stop believing in you.

No matter if your steps are big or small, keep stepping, because you are almost there

Daily Exercise — "A Note to Self"

Step 1: Take a moment to tell yourself how proud you are of YOU!

Step 2: Write a short letter to yourself expressing your love and gratitude for you. You must include the five words listed below

Step 3: Create a journal entry expressing how this made you feel.

1. Love
2. Enough
3. Grateful
4. Proud
5. Thankful

Strut Talk

Date _____

Why Try To Fit In When You Were Created To Stand Out

Are you spending your time trying to be what you see instead of being who you are? If this is you, it stops today!

Today is a new day to love and appreciate yourself like only you can. You will not spend another moment yearning for the approval and acceptance of others. From this moment forward, you will live the unapologetic life that is filled with endless possibilities and opportunities that we all deserve as individuals.

You will live free and fearless. It is time to get comfortable standing out and spending less time trying to conform to what society views as normal, attractive, and acceptable. Learning to love yourself as you are and for who you are is the perfect way to teach others how to love and respect you.

Own that thing that makes you "Different" - that thing that makes you, YOU and share it with the world. Do not be afraid to be you. Stand firm in your uniqueness and make them want to know your name. There is nothing more attractive than a person who knows and accepts who they are

Daily Exercise — Challenge Your Inner Critic

Most of the negative thoughts that we have about our image are not our true feelings. They are based off the opinions of others and we end up believing them. That stops today.

Step 1: Write a list of the things that you love about yourself and explain why

Step 2: Write a list of things that you do not like about yourself and explain why not

Step 3: Compare the two lists and answer the following questions:

1. Do you not like these things about yourself or has the world made you feel this way?

2. Do you believe that you were perfectly made?

3. Are you ready to embrace the true version of yourself?

Step 4: Replace your negative thoughts about yourself in Step 2: with positive thoughts

Step 5: Create a journal entry describing how this made you feel

Strut Talk

Date _____

Fall In Love With Yourself And The Rest Will Follow

Did you know that learning to fall in love with yourself is vital to your own happiness?

When you fall in love, you put yourself in position to receive that same love in return. One of the first steps to loving yourself is to take the steps necessary to feel and heal from your pain. When we do not address our hurt and past trauma, it grows and will cause you to lose love and respect for yourself (as well as others), often causing you to feel like you are not good enough or less than. The truth is…. you are more than enough!

It is bad enough that we must deal with negativity from others, but what about when we speak negative to ourselves and then expect something positive in return? We cannot expect to receive something that we're not even willing to give to ourselves. Start taking the time to forgive and love on yourself, whether it is positive self-talk, meditation, quiet time, or by simply setting boundaries.

When you truly make the decision to start loving yourself, you will feel more in control of your life and happiness. You will no longer seek the approval or attention from others due to your true satisfaction with yourself. You will put yourself in position to build stronger relationships in your business and personal lives. Practicing self-love is needed to be able to strut through life's challenges and live a life that is filled with purpose and happiness. Once you do this, you will attract the same love that you are.

Stop comparing yourself to others. Half of what we see is not always what it appears to be

Daily Exercise - Mirror Talk

Step 1: Find a quiet and safe space with a mirror and have a self-love conversation with yourself!

Step 2: Take 1 minute to "Fall in love with the person you see"

Step 3: As you are looking into your own eyes, I want you to smile at the person who is looking back at you and repeat the following 10 affirmations listed below:

1. I am proud of you
2. You are more than enough
3. I forgive you
4. You are worthy of love
5. I am in love with who I see
6. You are the greatest form of love
7. You are the love that you desire
8. True love lives inside of you
9. My love for you is unconditional
10. I am Love

Step 4: Create a Journal entry explaining in detail how this made you feel

Strut Talk

Date _____

Today Is A New Day - Live In It

Yesterday is gone forever and tomorrow is not promised. Those are two things that we know for sure, but often we get so caught up in the yesterdays and tomorrows that we forget about "Today"

This is my reminder to you.

You cannot spend another moment complaining about what happened to you yesterday or putting things off that need to be done today until tomorrow. You were blessed with this brand new day to live.

Today is your new day to release your limitations and create a new version of what your happiness looks and feels like. Today is the perfect day for you to get one step closer to reaching your goals and making your hopes and dreams your reality. Today is a brand new day to create memories and leave lasting impressions.

Today is your fresh start at life and a new day to live, love, learn and grow. Today is your new day to forgive and be forgiven. Today is your new day to be grateful. Today is your new day to smile, laugh, dance, pray and watch your kids grow. Most importantly, today is a new day to say, "I love you" and so much more!

Let's start treating today as if it were the only day that existed and do this same thing tomorrow and all of the days to come. Don't get so caught up with what happened yesterday or what tomorrow holds that you miss out on the love, blessings and opportunities that are prepared for you today! Be grateful for today and your new opportunity to live your life with purpose and passion.

Today is your fresh start to the rest of your life.... Live it!!

Daily Exercise - "Smell The Cake & Blow Out The Candles"

Step 1: Close your eyes and imagine that your favorite freshly baked cake is in front of you.

Step 2: Slowly smell the cake. Make sure to take a deep breath. As you inhale, imagine that you're inhaling everything that you want and deserve into your life. Hold for 4 seconds,

Step 3: Slowly blow out the candles with a 6 second exhale. Imagine that you are releasing everything that no longer serves a purpose in your life.

Step 4: Repeat this four times

Step 5: In your journal create an entry expressing how this exercise made you feel using 3-5 sentences.

Strut Talk   Date_____

_____
_____
_____
_____
_____
_____
_____
_____
_____
_____
_____
_____
_____
_____
_____
_____
_____
_____
_____
_____
_____
_____
_____
_____
_____
_____
_____
_____
_____
_____
_____
_____
_____

It No Longer Belongs To You - You Can Let It Go!

No one is really taught how to heal from trauma, so it is scary. When traumatic situations happen in our lives, we cannot believe that it happened to us. Oftentimes, we ask the question "why me" or "how will I get through this"? We end up isolating ourselves from the world due to feeling alone, fear of judgement, or feeling ashamed of what we are going through or have been through. This causes us to suffer in silence.

We can no longer allow the actions of hurt people to hold us hostage, especially knowing that "HURT PEOPLE, HURT PEOPLE". Consider this: That thing that happened to you as a child or the situation that you may be going through in this moment right now is no reflection of who you are now. You are not required to carry that burden of heaviness. You can free yourself by not giving it power and control in your life. It doesn't belong to you!

It's time to stop allowing these situations to dictate your happiness. Grow from them.

Accepting and forgiving your past hurt, pain and trauma is important. Once you forgive, it will no longer be able to hurt you.

It's time to break generational cycles of trauma. It can start with you!

Daily Exercise - "Gone For Good"

Step 1: Write a list of at least 5 things/situations that have hurt you in the (past or present)

Step 2: Answering the following questions.

1. Has it been forgiven?

2. Are you willing /ready to give?

3. Forgive (if you're ready)

Step 3: Release it by simply BURNING IT!

Step 4: In a fireplace or safe space, burn your list or hurt. Just like that, it's gone.

Step 5: Do this as often as needed until the need longer exists

Step 6: Create a journal entry describing how this made you feel

Strut Talk

Date _____

You Have Yourself To Remind You Of Love

Have you been looking for love in all the wrong places?

Most of us will spend a lifetime searching for love and approval from others, not realizing that true love is closer than we think. It's inside of us! We are the love for which we are searching! Self-love causes you to be at peace and proud of yourself, regardless of what you have been through or are going through. It is about letting go of the limited beliefs that have been forced in your life, knowing, and believing that you are perfectly made and that you are the greatest form of love.

Many of us are searching for love because of the lack of love, affection, and attention that we may have received as children. We grow up desperately trying to fill that "Love Void." We try to fill it with relationships/friendships, work, food, shopping, sex, drugs, or other things that are supposed to distract our attention and make us feel good. Don't get me wrong! We all want something that makes us feel good, but we must be careful to not get caught up with temporary satisfaction. Just because something feels good does not mean that it's good for us. Once that feeling is gone, we end of feeling worse and even more alone. We rely on other people to remind us of love and our greatness and end up being disappointed, instead of reminding ourselves.

The next time you are feeling unloved or unappreciated, I want you to fill your own "love void" by giving praise to yourself. Make it a habit of telling yourself how proud you are of yourself. Treat yourself out to a beautiful dinner. Get dressed up just because. Facilitate a random act of kindness. These small gestures amplify your love for self. The more love you show, the more love you will receive in return.

Daily Exercise - Love Wins

Place one or both hands over your heart. Rest them there for a few deep breaths. Repeat the following self-love mantras.

(Feel free to add your own)

- I am human

- I am strong, I am beautiful, and I am worthy of that same love

- I will fill my heart with love and gratitude every day

- I remind myself daily that I am enough

- Just breathe

- Today and every day I will show myself love, patience and kindness

- I accept and love myself exactly as I am.

- I can fill my own love void

Strut Talk

Date _____

Turn Your Pain Into Power

We all have or will experience some form of pain throughout this lifetime. Whether it be grief caused by the loss of a loved one, heartbreak from a relationship or disappointment, it is going to happen.

During these moments, we must learn how to allow ourselves to feel those heavy emotions to heal and regain our strength. When my son was killed, there was nothing that anyone could have said to make me believe that things would get better. I was so consumed with my heartache and pain. I felt as if there was no way out! I began to feel like a hostage to my own feelings and emotions, causing me to remain in a very dark place - a place that I knew I did not want to be.

Then, I started thinking about my purpose in life, as well as his and knew that I had to make a choice.

1. Continue to walk in the hurt and pain allowing it to dictate my peace and happiness causing me to be bitter?

Or

2. Trust God and grow from it, allowing it to make me better?

This was the hardest decision that I have ever had to make not just as a mother, but as a person. I realized in that moment that I held the power to re-author my story. I realized in those moments that my love for my sun was greater than the pain I felt. I knew that I had to keep going for him. I found a level of power and strength inside of me that I never knew existed.

He Became My Why!

I don't know the darkness that you are going through, but I want to remind you that the same power resides inside of you! You may not see the strength in your situation, but if you take the necessary steps to heal, remain optimistic and allow the universe to make things clear for you, you will! When you trust the process and understand that your life is written, you begin to view challenging times as chapters in your book called "Life". On the other side of pain, there is power that teaches us empathy and gives us a stronger desire to forgive, love, and understand and turn our pain around.

Embrace your pain by sharing your story of survival with the world. You will give hope to others and power to yourself!

Feel the pain till it hurts no more ~ Shakespeare

Daily Exercise - "What Is Your Why?"

Take a moment to simply remind yourself of how you were able to strut thru some of life's most difficult challenges and answer the following questions in your journal.

1. What was/is your why?

2. What steps did you take to heal?

3. Has your why changed? If so, how?

4. Did you find power through your pain?

5. How are you using that power to impact the world?

Strut Talk

Date_____

Be The Change You Want To See

We can no longer complain and not be willing to be a part of the change. For things to change, we must be willing to do the same. Life is always going to be filled with the good, the bad, and the ugly! This is inevitable. We may not have any control over that, but we do have control over ourselves and the power within us to make the initial changes that start with each of us.

Without actions, things will always remain the same. They will not get better. When we make personal changes, we grow. We become the example of what we want to see and who we want to be. It starts with changing your mindset, your actions, your habits and eliminating limited beliefs.

Example: None of us want to be judged because of who we are, where we're from or what we've been through. That said, we should never we find ourselves judging others for those same reasons.

It's time for us to not only hold ourselves accountable, but also those connected to us. If you think you're doing everything right and you **witness** something that's **wrong** and you do **nothing**, you are a part of the **problem**! It's time that we all change, what we can, where we can, while we can.

Now, are we going to change the world overnight? Absolutely not! But we will be heading in the right direction.

Daily Exercise - "Out With The Old, In With The New"

Step 1: In your journal, write down 3 habits that you are committed to changing.

Step 2: What steps are you going to take to make these changes?

Step 3: Once you've changed them, how do you feel now?

Step 4: Journal the experience

Strut Talk

Date

M.O.D.E.L. : Mentor Others & Develop Eternal Love

When most of us think of the word model, we automatically think about fashion, beauty, or a New York City fashion show. What if we could change the perception and create a new reality when it comes to that word? To me, being a model has nothing has nothing to do with what you look like, but it has everything to do with our actions and what we put out to the world.

My definition of a model is anyone who mentors others while developing eternal love.

As a role model, we have the responsibility to **Mentor** those around us. We seek to encourage, guide, and lead them in the right direction. When we provide love and support to each other, it gives us a sense of purpose, helps put things into perspective and makes us feel better about our own life.

Others may consist of your friends, family, children, coworkers or even somebody that you do not know. If a person is put in your path and you see/feel that there is a need to build them up, your job is to do it! When we pour into those in need or connected to us, we assist with their healing and can help them to develop a greater love for self. Even when we do not know each other, we are still connected.

Developing self-love and trust allows us to experience ourselves in our greatest form. We become the new example of what love looks and feels like by creating a love that is unconditional, without limitation, and lasts forever.

Eternal Love, the most purist form of love, never ends. This love is so powerful that it lives on beyond you.

So, the next time someone ask, "are you a model?", tell them yes and let them know that the world is your Runway!

Daily Exercise - "Are You A Model Citizen?"

Many of us talk the talk, but are you walking the walk? Let's find out by answering the following questions

1. Are you doing your part as a leader to uplift and encourage those around you?

2. When you see something wrong, do you look away or speak up?

3. Do you stand firm in your truth?

4. Are you a role model and positive influence to others, even when you do not know them personally?

5. Do you practice self-love? If so, how?

6. Do you lead by example?

7. Are you a great listener and communicator?

8. Are you confident?

9. Do you have passion and an ability to inspire?

10. Are you selfless and accepting of others regardless of race, gender, religion?

Strut Talk

Date

You Can't Be Down When You're Standing Tall

Throughout this lifetime, many of us will experience hardships and difficult times causing us to feel like we have the weight of the world on our shoulders. During these moments, we often feel overwhelmed and filled with darkness. This allows those feelings to affect us mentally. They also have a strong effect on our physical demeanor also known as our body language.

Our minds and our bodies have such a powerful connection. Whatever the mind is feeling, the body communicates. For instance, if you are feeling depressed or sad about a situation that you are dealing with, your posture is probably going to be slouched over with your shoulders in and head down. This causes you to feel down and in a depressed or unhappy state of being.

By changing your posture, (shoulders back, chest out, chin up, core tight) your mind will follow, and you will begin to feel more confident and in control of your emotions. A few simple adjustments to your posture can improve your entire mood. When you change your posture, you change the narrative.

It's hard to be down when you're standing TALL! If you don't believe me, try it for yourself

Daily Exercise - Mirror Talk

Step 1: I want you to stand in front of a mirror and simply look at YOU!!

(Remember how you feel/write it down) Answer the following questions.

1. What do you see?

2. How do you feel?

3. What is your body language saying?

4. Do you feel confident or powerful?

Step 2: Change your body language and repeat the same thing! Answer the same questions.

- Shoulders Back

- Chest Out

- Chin up

- Core Tight

Compare the results of Step 1 and Step 2 - How do you feel?

Strut Talk

Date _____

Strut Thru It, Until You Get To It

Your journey to becoming a better YOU, will take time, faith and patience. It **WILL NOT** happen overnight. There will be many obstacles and challenges that are going to stand in your way, but you must keep going. These are the times to stand firm in your truth and remain resilient. You have the power to Strut Thru anything that comes your way - not just today, but every day.

Let's face it. Life is a battle. There are going to be many times that we get knocked down. We must find the strength within us to get back up, keep fighting and refuse to allow anyone or anything to stop us from reaching our greatest potential. The reason why many of us have not achieved our dreams is because we gave up when things got tough forgetting that we are TOUGHER!

You may experience times when you'll want to throw in the towel and give up, but don't! In this moment, remain humble and focused on the finish line. Do not focus on what's standing in our way. You must continue to Strut! You must put in the work and effort it takes to move forward, even when you don't want to and things seems impossible.

In order to get to it, you will have to Strut thru it!

Daily Exercise — Carry It With You

Step 1: Write down a recurring critical thought on a small piece of paper

Step 2: At the end of the day/week/month, I want you to look at them collectively and release them out of your life (discard, burn, whatever you decide)

Step 3: Write a journal entry expressing how this made you feel

Strut Talk   Date_____

_____
_____
_____
_____
_____
_____
_____
_____
_____
_____
_____
_____
_____
_____
_____
_____
_____
_____
_____
_____
_____
_____
_____
_____
_____
_____
_____
_____
_____
_____
_____
_____
_____
_____
_____
_____

I'm Perfect, Imperfect

Repeat after me - I'M PERFECT, IMPERFECT! (Say it louder for the people in the back)

Would you believe me if I told you that one of the main obstacles that is standing in the way of you finding your true happiness, is YOU? We spend too much time complaining about the things we want to change about ourselves, overlooking the fact that each of us are perfectly made, hence the title of this mantra, I'm Perfect, Imperfect.

This is the proof that our imperfections are what make us unique. It's the thing that sets us apart from the rest. Many of us are missing out on true happiness within ourselves because we're too focused on what it looks like instead of putting the emphasis on what happiness feels like. Just because something looks perfect on the outside doesn't mean that it is. We all want to be the best version of who we are and the only way to truly do that is to start loving and embracing our imperfections.

When I was growing up, I hated so many things about myself. One day, I realized that those feelings were forced on me by people who were unhappy with themselves. The exact things that I grew up not liking about myself are now the things that I adore most about myself. I had to learn to love and accept every part of me and to stop allowing the opinions of others to affect the love I had for myself.

Once you're able to do this, you will fall in love with yourself. Others will feel that love and respond. Be proud of who you are, what you look like, where you're from, where you've been and finally where you're going. Your life was designed for you. Everything about you is one of a kind.

Today is a new day to remind yourself that you are perfectly made!

Now repeat after me - **"I'M PERFECT, IMPERFECT"**

Daily Exercise - "Crush On You"

Most of us are great with complimenting others. When was the last you took the time to compliment yourself?

Step 1: I want you to take a moment and really look at yourself from a place of self-love, value and appreciation.

Step 2: I want you to embrace everything you see.

Step 3: Write down as many self-compliments as possible within 1min. (This must be timed because I do not want you to over think.)

Step 4: Journal how this experience made you feel

Strut Talk

Date _____

S. T.R.U. T—
Stand Tall Revealing Your
Unadulterated Truth

Did you know that your strut was the first conversation that you had with the world? Even when we use no words, our body language and eye contact do the talking for us. Instead of walking in life's challenge's allowing them to dictate our happiness, we must remember that we have the power to either walk in it or strut thru it.

When you make the decision to strut through life, you are fearlessly accepting ownership as to who you are by standing tall in your truth and not being afraid to reveal it to the world. Many of us are still hostage to the shame and guilt of our past hurt and trauma. That ends in this moment. It's time to reclaim your power, starting with embracing your truth: the good, the bad and the ugly.

We can no longer compromise our healing process by living a lie. The pretending stops now! Share your truth regardless of how difficult it may be. By standing in your truth, you are being the example to others that you can turn your pain into power! What you've survived has made you a better, YOU!

Daily Exercise - "Reveal And Be Free"

It's time to reveal your truth!

Have been holding on to any negative feelings regarding a person, situation, or decision?

Are you not being honest with those around you due to the fear of judgment?

Are you ready to free yourself?

How did this make you feel? Do you feel free?

Strut Talk

Date _____

The World Is Your Runway, 6, 7, Strut !!

Even when we do not want to be put on display, the world is always watching and trying to figure out who we are. It's so important to make sure you're putting your best foot forward. As you Strut through life today, I want you to first make sure that you're in position.

1. Shoulders back

2. Chest out

3. Chin up

Now I want you to focus your mind on your inner strength and personal growth. As you take each step, I want you to think about the obstacles and challenges that you have overcome to get to where you are today. As you stand tall embracing YOU, I want you to be proud of who you are, where you've been and especially where you're headed. There's no one greater than you!

You have stood tall through your most difficult moments, even when you didn't think you had the strength to do so. Converse with the world today. Re-introduce yourself allowing your strut to have the conversation for you. Put your confidence, ownership and uniqueness on display today as you strut with power, purpose and passion. Be proud of your journey! Regardless of what comes your way today, you will remain resilient, graceful and focused on your happiness.

Life is too precious to simply walk in it! Be Bold! Be Beautiful! Last, but not least, BE YOU!

In the words of Coco Chanel "Every day Is a Fashion Show and The World Is Your Runway"

Daily Exercise - "Strut Like The Entire World Is Watching"

Let's have some fun today as you Strut through life!

Step 1: First, get yourself in position.

1. Shoulders back

2. Chest out

3. Chin up

Step 2: Think about where you're headed in life.

Step 3: Now, I want you to Strut towards your happiness with power, authority, grace, and ownership. It doesn't matter if you're walking down an aisle, hallway, through your home or office, outside, or in the grocery store! Strut!

I want you to answer the following questions.

1. How did this make you feel?

2. How did people respond to you?

3. What did you enjoy about this?

4. What was your biggest fear?

5. Are you ready to commit to strutting through life?

Strut Talk

Date _____

These Are Just Chapters, Not The End Of Your Story

I want to stop for just a moment and reflect on the many obstacles that you have had to overcome in your life. Many would say, "don't look back", but I am a firm believer that looking back is the only way to see how far you have come. Furthermore, it is confirmation that you are no longer there! We must start looking at life as a book. Every obstacle or situation that you have gone through has been a "Chapter" in your life story. There will be good chapters as well as bad chapters. Together, they all shape you into who you are or want to become.

Through each chapter you will learn and grow. You will become wiser and stronger, and your previous chapters will become clear. We will gain an understanding about your purpose and why these situations ("Chapters") were written. It's time to embrace your chapters. Without each of these moments, you wouldn't be who you are today. Some of your most horrible chapters shaped you into the person that you are today.

Be grateful for your chapters as you grow from each lesson. Prepare yourself for the chapters ahead.

Strut Talk

Date _____

Today Is Filled My Endless Possibilities

You should be so excited about today! Do you realize how blessed you are to have a brand new day to live, love, laugh and experience life? This is your new day to take back your power and regain yourself control and confidence. Do not waste another minute worrying about the "what ifs" when you can focus on "what is" and "what will be".

Today is a new day to make your mark on the world by turning your dreams into your new reality. This is the time to get excited about the new possibilities that are waiting for you - both seen and unseen. Today is a new day to remind yourself of your greatness. You are worthy of every opportunity and possibility that is coming in your direction! Use this new day to turn your problems into possibilities.

Stop allowing negative thoughts and people to keep you stagnant while missing the opportunities that are waiting for you. Surround yourself with people who are going to push you towards your possibilities, not hold you back from them. If you do not have a support system, push your damn self! Stay focused on what is in front of you. That's all there is to see!

Now, strut thru this beautiful day that was prepared for you! Put all your faith in believing that today is going to be an amazing day filled with endless possibilities.

You know who you are and what you're made of! OWN IT and STOP playing with yourself!

Daily Exercise - Out With The Old. In With The New (Way Of Thinking)

Step 1: In your Self Love journal, I want you to write the words "Negative Thoughts" on one side and draw a line in between. On the opposite side, write the words "Positive Thoughts".

Step 2: Now, I want you to write down 5 negative thoughts that you have when it comes to fulfilling your dreams, goals and possibilities.

Step 3: Then on the opposite side, I want you to replace those negative thoughts with "Positive self-Talk".

(Example Below)

Negative Thoughts	Positive Thoughts
I have never accomplished anything in my life.	I have accomplished many things in my life.
I am a failure.	I am a success.
I'm not smart enough .	I am intelligent on all levels.
I am not worthy.	I am more than worthy.

Strut Talk

Date _____

It's Ok To Not Be Ok With What You've Been Allowing In Your Life!!

Dear Self,

Today is the day to put your foot down and regain your power and ownership! You will no longer settle when it comes to your happiness or the things that you are willing to accept in your life. You have been pretending that things are "ok" for way too long and its stops today!

Do you know why people have been mistreating you? .... because you have taught them how to by continuously allowing them to get away with things with which you are not ok. The reason that many of us have this issue is because we have gotten use to settling to satisfy others or "keep the peace" instead of standing for what we genuinely believe and want in our lives.

We have gotten comfortable and stuck in the "it is what it is" mentality and it is not ok. It is time to use your voice and no longer feel powerless when it comes to setting standards for yourself. You have gotten way too silent when it comes to speaking up for what you want and deserve in your life. The time to stand tall and start setting boundaries for your life is NOW! Start with teaching people how to treat you.

If you are not ok with something, say it! If they cannot respect your feelings, you must be willing to let them go until they do. This pertains to friends, family, spouse, children, co-workers, strangers...... EVERYBODY!

The time has come for you to speak up for yourself and to stop allowing toxic people to rob you of your peace and happiness. The only person that can change the way people treat you, is you.

Daily Exercise - "It Stops Today"

Step 1: In your journal I want you to write a list of the things that you have been allowing in your life that you are not ok with.

Step 2: From whom are you allowing this? (Be honest with yourself)

Step 3: What boundaries have you set to make sure this treatment does not continue?

Step 4: How has this made you feel and/or affected your relationships?

Strut Talk

Date _____

You Will Never Know Who You Are Unless You Free Yourself From Who You Pretend To Be

Are you familiar with the saying "real recognizes real"? Well, I am here to tell you that real also recognizes "fake".

The time has come to stop pretending and realize that the only person that you are fooling is yourself!! It is bad enough that we must wear mask to remain safe in the world today. Many of us have been wearing masks to hide our identity daily by trying to fit in. We have covered up who we truly are often feeling like we are not good enough. The truth is, we are more than enough!

We find ourselves overwhelmed and stressed out trying to live up to the expectations and standards of others and trying to do what they do instead of just doing "you." It is time to follow your own path and stop comparing your journey to the journey of others. No two journeys are the same. Stop being afraid of being you. It is time to remove the mask and reintroduce yourself.

We all have insecurities about our self-image. Even the individuals that we are pretending to be like are insecure about their self-image. Embrace your truth and stop pretending to be what/who you are not. It is time to let the world know who you truly are, what you are made of and what you stand for.

The only way for you to make genuine connections and have meaningful relationships is to accept your truth and let go of your ego.

People connect with authenticity, not fakeness. Give yourself the credit that you deserve. Trust yourself and the rest will follow. There is an entire world of opportunity waiting for the authentic you. Now go get it!

Remember, it is not about who you are, what you look like, or what you have been through. It is about who you aspire to become!

Daily Exercise — Who Are You Versus Who You Want To Be

Step 1: I want you to take a moment to answer the question "Who are you"?

Step 2: Write down as many positive qualities about yourself as possible in 1 minute (Set your timer)

Step 3: Who are you pretending to be? (Be honest with yourself)

Step 4: Now, I want you to compare the answers to both questions and create a plan to become everything that you are pretending to be.

Step 5: Journal this experience

Strut Talk

Date

Just Smile

No matter what comes your way today, SMILE!

You have allowed life and your current situation to keep you frowning for way too long. Stop moping around and beating yourself up about the things that you can no longer change. Take advantage of this new opportunity to put a smile on your beautiful face because you deserve it. If you cannot find the strength to do it for yourself, do it for someone else. We all are trying to figure out the formula to strutting thru tough times. Oftentimes, we overlook the fact that a simple smile can be part of the solution.

Many of us are guilty of allowing life's challenges to keep us in a space of uncertainty and often afraid to smile because we feel as if we do not deserve to. It does not matter what you are going through or have experienced in the past, everyone deserves to smile. The fact that you are alive and have more life to live is reason enough!

You have been blessed with a new day to live, to be greater, to grow wiser and spread love. If that is not a reason to smile, I do not know what is. As you smile today, I want you to feel proud for taking care of yourself. This small act of self-love that can add light to the darkest situations, not only for you, but also for those around you.

A smile may seem simple to most, but it is one of the most powerful weapons that you have. It is time for you to use it!

If you find yourself in a not so happy mood today, replace what you are feeling with a smile. Hold yourself accountable for putting a smile on someone else's face today and watch how good it makes you feel.

Daily Exercise - "Smile For Me"

I want you intentionally do something nice to put a smile on someone's face today.

1. Give a compliment to someone who deserves it.

2. Pay it forward (pay for someone's lunch or another item)

3. Smile to at least 3 random people until they smile back.

4. Journal the experience. How did this make you feel? Did you smile? Did they smile?

Strut Talk

Date _____

Grow Thru What You Go Thru

One thing that we know for sure is that life is not always going to be peaches and cream. We are guaranteed to make mistakes, bad decisions, and experience hardships no matter how hard we try to avoid them. There will be challenging moments that are beyond our control that will make us want to come out on the other side, but that is far from the truth. Our toughest moments are also some of the greatest lessons in life. It's in these moments that we realize what we are made of.

Of course, we all would like to live a life without trials and tribulations. Would that really be life?

Every situation that we have or will experience in this lifetime is designed to help us to grow in some shape or form. When we survive them, it confirms that what does not kill us will indeed make us stronger. This can be mentally, emotionally, physically, or spiritually. Tough times will not last forever. You will get through them if you believe. No matter how many times you get knocked down, remember that you have the power within you to get back up.

Embrace your struggles knowing that your most painful moments will strengthen you and that you will come out on the other side.

In the words of Aaliyah, "if at first you don't succeed, dust yourself off and try again"

Daily Exercise - Gratitude Jar

Step 1: Find a jar or box

Step 2: Decorate the jar however you like

Step 3: This is the most crucial step that will be repeated daily or as often as needed. Think of no less than three things that you are grateful for (big or small) write them down on a small slip of paper and fill your jar. These will be known as gratitude notes.

During moments that you feel down, or life gets overwhelming, pull out a few of your gratitude notes. Read them to remind yourself of the people, places, and things that you are grateful for.

Step 4: Journal how this makes you feel

Strut Talk

Date _____

_____
_____
_____
_____
_____
_____
_____
_____
_____
_____
_____
_____
_____
_____
_____
_____
_____
_____
_____
_____
_____
_____
_____
_____
_____
_____
_____
_____
_____
_____
_____
_____
_____
_____
_____

Use It Before You Lose It

We are all born with a special talent, gift, or creative ability. Many of us are very connected to these gifts and use them as a source of self-expression and inspiration to not only create but to get through tough times. There are others who have allowed life's challenges to dim the light on their passion that once shined bright. When life gets complicated, we are quick to put the things that we love on hold and wait for that perfect moment or opportunity. When we stop using our potential, we risk the chance of losing it. Without practice and use, your ability can slowly fade. Practice can be that missing puzzle piece/gap between you, your goals and overall success. It can make the difference between good and great.

Start using our abilities and get back to what makes you happy.

Daily Exercise - "Get Back To It"

Step 1: In your journal, I want you to create a list of your creative talents (singing, dancing, voice, writing, painting, etc.)

Step 2: Write down the last time you were able to use your skills or talents.

Step 3: Answer the following question

1. What caused you to stop expressing your creativity?

Step 4: Make a commitment to yourself to get back to it

Step 5: What steps will you take to make this happen

Strut Talk

Date _____

Let God, Let Go, Live Life, Layla

Have you truly forgiven your past or are you still allowing it to hold you hostage? If you are, trust me. You're not alone. Many of us are guilty of allowing our past to negatively affect our current/present happiness and outlook on life. We find ourselves fighting a no-win battle, constantly struggling, and trying to find the strength within to strut thru these tough times. In these moments, we often feel lost, alone, and hopeless, and like we have the weight of the world on our shoulders. To say it's heavy would be an understatement. In these exact moments, it is important for us to understand that these battles do not belong to us! These are the times to remain faithful beyond our understanding and to keep going!

I want to take this time to remind **YOU** that **YOU** hold the POWER within to activate your own happiness, but you don't have to do it alone. Today is the perfect day to **Let God** into your heart and allow Him to help heal your mind, body and soul.

> *The Lord shall fight for you, and ye shall hold your peace.*
> **Exodus 14:14 (KJV)**

Today is the perfect day to **Let Go of what's been holding you back and redirect your** focus on this new beginning. It's time to free yourself of the feelings and emotions caused by failures and disappointments in your life and understand that they were all just lessons. We all face moments that set us back (relationships/break-ups, betrayal, abuse, grief, illness, life, etc.) but this doesn't mean that we can't come back better and stronger. We can no longer allow these situations to cause us to become bitter. It's time for us to face our truth, free ourselves and allow these situations to make us better.

> *Trust in the Lord with all thine heart; and lean not unto thine own understanding.*
>
> *In all thy ways acknowledge him, and he shall direct thy paths.*
>
> **Proverbs 3:5-6 (KJV)**

Today and every day moving forward, you will **Live Life** on purpose and be intentional about creating your own happiness. It's time to make the most out of this 1 life that we have. It's time to start looking at each day as a fresh start, a new beginning. It's time to be true to who you are and stop putting your focus on pleasing others. Stop complaining about the things you cannot change and start changing the things that you can. It's time to live!!

> *And now abideth faith, hope, charity, these three; but the greatest of these is charity.*
>
> **1 Corinthians 13:13 (KJV)**

Last, but not least, **LAYLO** – focus on your life and creating your version of happiness and stop worrying about what others think or are doing. Create your own lane and STAY IN IT! Take good care of yourself, your mind, body, and soul. Be selective as to who shares your energy. Set standards. Talk less and listen more. Become exclusive, yet remain humble and approachable. Finally, and most importantly, MIND YOUR OWN BUSINESS!!

> *Surely he scorneth the scorners: but he giveth grace unto the lowly.*
>
> **Proverbs 3:34 (KJV)**

Daily Exercise — "It Was Already Written"

Step 1: Take a moment to reference the highlighted verses

Step 2: In your journal, I want you to write out the entire meaning of each verse. Meditate on it and connect it to your life in this moment

Step 3: Next, I want you to speak it over your life and understand that this is already written for YOU! There is a "word" for every situation that we will face in this lifetime. We don't have to figure this out on our own.

Step 4: Write a Journal entry expressing how this made you feel

Strut Talk

Date _____

Strut Talk Affirmations

I Am Love and all the love I need is inside of me!

I Am My own vibe of positive energy!

I Am Worthy of greatness!

I Am Prepared to receive the love!

I Am Healing on a daily basis!

I Am Full of potential!

I Am Grateful for every moment in my life!

I Am Flawless because of my Flaws

I Am Not my past hurt and trauma!

I Am Confident in my skin!

I Am Forgiving!

I Am My own voice of reason!

I Am The light that is needed to get through my darkness!

I Am ME and I love it!

I Am What power and authority look like!

I Am Excited about today!

I Am Excited about today!

I Am Strong!

I Am Capable!

I Am A Blessing to this world as well as myself!

I Am Patient with me and those around me!

I Am Understanding!

I Am Ok with not being ok and that's OK!

I Am Not my failures. They are no reflection of me!

I Am Fearless!

I Am Beautifully Made!

I Am Excited about today!

I Am Happy, and it feels so good!

I Am More than my body!

I Am Unique, one of a kind!

I Am Bold and Beautiful!

I Am Giving to those in need!

I Am Encouraging to myself first!

I Am Sensitive, kind and funny!

I Am A creator of my creativity

I Am Wise and filled with Wisdom!

I Am Deserving of the Best!

I Am Youthful!

I Am Proud of myself and the person I am becoming!

I Am Resilient!

I Am Made with greatness!

I Am Constantly improving!

I Am The change that I want to see in this world!

I Am A leader, but will also follow!

I Am My brother's keeper!

I Am Humble!

I Am My sisters' keeper!

I Am Smart and still learning!

I Am Perfect, imperfect!

I Am Free from anxiety!

I Am A survivor, who will continue to survive!

I Am Wealth in abundance!

I Am More than enough!

I Am Open to love and support!

I Am Struttin' in my truth and its feels amazing!

ABOUT THE AUTHOR

~Lolita Frazier~

Lolita Frazier grew up in Williamsburg, VA, and is the oldest of four sisters. She was raised by a single mother and her grandmother, affectionally known as "Granny". Lolita, like many of us, grew up in an environment that wasn't always healthy and was forced to deal with many situations that caused her fear, anger, and self-doubt as a young girl. Being the oldest of her siblings and the only child to have a different father, she often found herself alone and misunderstood as a child. She considered herself the "black sheep" in her family. She dealt with many feelings of rejection and abandonment due to not knowing her birth father and grew up allowing those feelings and emotions to dictate her happiness.

Her mother, a woman she described as a beautiful kind, yet feisty soul, was her protector and role model. She was known and respected by many for her unique sense of style, her passion for fashion, and her ability to light up any room she entered with her vibrant personality. Lolita naturally found herself following in her mother's footsteps, eventually developing that same love for herself as well as fashion. She often found herself daydreaming of one day being like the super models in the Vogue fashion magazines that her mother not only collected but cherished

Lolita's mother constantly reassured her that she was loved and beautiful. She always reminded her that the hurt she faced as a child was no reflection of her, but instead they were just the actions of "hurt people".

By the time Lolita reached her teenage years, she began to develop that same love for herself and those negative feelings she had experienced as a child slowly began to fade. She gained an understanding about "hurt people, hurt people". She began to look at her life as a story and realized that those moments were only chapters, not the end of her story. She realized that she had to experience a lot to become the person she was destined to be.

As an adult, Lolita turned those daydreams into her reality by becoming a model that graces runways around the world. She is best known for her swift yet graceful ability to tell her a story thru her "strut". Her narrative had changed. It was no longer a story about her beauty or even about being a model. This was her way of struttin' thru every life challenge that she had ever experienced. The runway would become her outlet - a place to connect, release, inspire and finally be able to stand in her truth. She had finally reached her happiness and then... she found herself dealing with the hurt yet again.

In 2016, Lolita experienced the greatest pain that any mother would experience when she received the phone call that her only Sun, Jordan, was murdered at the hands of a hurt person. Her heart stopped. In that moment, Lolita found herself numb to say the least and began to feel hostage to her thoughts, feelings, and emotions. She frequently asked the question "why me?". She had spent a lifetime healing from her childhood trauma and now this. Lolita found herself in a very dark place. She was ready to give up, but then she remembered her mother's lessons. As horrible as this was, it was just another chapter and not the end of her story. Lolita had two choices: do I "walk in" this pain and allow it to take me out causing me to be bitter or do I "strut thru it" knowing that God is in control?

SHE CHOSE TO STRUT THRU IT!

Her work has been published, recognized, and featured on national and international levels.

- Penn Medicine Documentary
  - "Runway to Recovery" (Youtube)
  - "Not Just One" - A documentary about metastatic breast cancer w/AnaOno Intimates @NYFW Featured in Glamour.com
- SIU School of Medicine
  - "Angels Amongst us"
- Lead Trainer Confidence Coach for Project Cancerland @ NYFW
- Runway Of Hope | Pink Warrior Angels TX (Story featured in Cove Leader Express)
- Cuidar International Publication Sintra, Portugal

Lolita Frazier is a runway therapist, confidence coach and the M.O.D.E.L citizen that uses the art of runway walking as a form of IMpowerment. This art helps hurt people strut thru their pain. Through her world-class runway training and model development institution, Loco Strut Runway, she administers her signature services: Strictly Strut (a runway certification program) and Strut Talk Runway Therapy, a thriving 501C3 nonprofit and a one-of-a-kind program that fuses runway walking and talk therapy

Lolita Frazier is a master communicator with a strong and unique ability to connect with others. Through her training her clients become more confident, graceful, and agile on their feet, creating both happiness and opportunity in their lives. Lolita shares her personal story of survival to give others strength and hope to be able to move forward after the loss of a loved one or any traumatic situation that has been faced. Lolita has influenced many people to become more self-aware of their emotions and how it shapes their body language and the story it tells the world. Lolita has a keen understanding that we all go through painful experiences. Lolita firmly believes that there are only two types of people in this world - people who walk in pain and people who strut thru it. We all have a story. Lolita has one question for you.

What does your strut say about you?

CPSIA information can be obtained
at www.ICGtesting.com
Printed in the USA
BVHW042347020422
632964BV00008B/179

9 781088 023853